ENOUGH

ENOUGH

ABIGAIL CULBERTSON

ISBN: 979-8-9866285-8-5

Author's Note

Within these pages, I speak a lot about whether what I felt was ever real. What makes our feelings real is never what other people make of them or where they came from, but the simple fact that we felt them at all. We all see the world through our own lens. What is real for you may not be real for me. I didn't always recognize that, but I do now. This was all real because I experienced it. I wrote it. It's my truth, and I want to remind you that your truth is valid too.

This was once a story inspired by real people. Arguably, all stories are just collages put together through inspirations of real people. But I'd like to note, this telling is mine. And I've pieced it together in the way that I'd like. This book is only one foggy window into a house full of memories, dreams, experiences, and imaginations. It's one of my favorite ones. But it is only one.

That said, I am so glad that I get to open it to all of you. I hope it inspires you to be passionate and brave in the way that you love, and in the way that you heal. I hope that it inspires you to indulge in everything that life has to offer you. And then I hope that you share and express every bit of it. Let it pour out of you in whatever way it wants to be known. Because darling, your love deserves to be seen.

Content Warning

This book contains sensitive material relating to:

Suicide
Self-harm
Depression
Anxiety
Homophobia
Emotional Abuse
Alcohol/drug use
Offensive language
Death/dying
Sexual/intimate content

Foreword

I think you can tell a lot about a person by how they answer the question, "Is love enough?" The fairytale believers will say yes. The non-believers, no. But then there are the in-betweens. Because once upon a time, I did believe. I believed so much that I wanted to make you prove it. I always wanted you to understand my story. To truly know me, thinking that knowing was the currency of love. Feeling seen is validating, yes. But validation is not equivalent to love. I know now, you did absolutely love me. You loved me more than I loved myself, and that is why I crumbled so swiftly when I could not feel your love. I wanted to not just know of your love, but to feel it too.

Here is the secret… there is not one other person on this planet that can make you feel love. It is physiologically impossible to experience the love of another person if you do not believe you are deserving of that love. If you cannot feel this love yourself. Put simply, when you are drowning you are so focused on survival that there is not a thing you can see or hear other than your own struggle for air. I could not let go of you when it felt like you were the only air I could find, the only way I could hang on to myself. Holding on to you so tight was one of the biggest mistakes I could have made, because when I finally lost you, all that was left was the water in my lungs. Consumed by the idea of you and the ever-questioning doubt, I had to find my way out, without you.

I needed a place to heal. A place to both love you and hate you. To yearn and to grieve. So, I wrote. I wrote letters and journal entries, poems, and songs. I wrote every word I left unsaid and gave myself the closure I needed by exposing my own truth. I never wrote any of this for her, the girl I loved more than anything else. I wrote it for me, the woman so deserving of all of the love that I had left to give. And now I am sharing this with all of you. I hope you find your own truth before trying to find someone else's. And I beg of you, do not ask others to find you before you can find yourself. Outward love is not enough. You deserve to feel that love too.

You are enough.

Contents

Love Without Question   1

The Beginning of the End   15

Betrayal   25

Pretending   35

Abandonment   55

Return   83

Yearning   105

Enough.   137

LOVE WITHOUT QUESTION
(P.S. It was short lived.)
(P.P.S. But it was beautiful while it lasted.)

Because I got to love you more
than I've loved anyone else
in this entire world.
And that,
was a magical thing.

I told the stars all I wanted
was to be happy.
That's when they brought me you.

The funny thing is… I don't actually remember when we truly became friends. But maybe that was always the point. It was meant to be natural. So, call it karma or not, I choose to believe that there was someone that always knew we were destined to be brought together. When I asked the universe for the things that I wanted, I wasn't sure it was listening. But looking back at it now, I realize that is why it gave me you. As it turns out, all I needed was a best friend by my side and I am so grateful that that best friend is you. Around you I feel like sunshine, and on the days I don't, I feel like the moon. Because just like the moon, I still reflect light. Your sunshine pours through me, illuminating every dark night. I would be lost without you.

You are my best friend because nobody on this planet has ever made me feel as important as you do. You believe in me and inspire me every day. So hear me when I say this, I believe in you too. With my whole self, and I want the absolute world for you. You taught me what a good relationship is. You loved me enough that I finally feel it too.

- The first letter.

I wasn't looking for love when I found you.
Actually, it was the quite the opposite.
I was terrified of the idea of letting someone in.
Terrified I couldn't love right,
or enough...
But you taught me there was nothing to fear
when it was easy sharing my world with you.
Easy sharing a bed.
Easy sharing my thoughts.
Easy sharing my time.
I think the only thing I found difficult was sharing my heart.
And I wonder how much of that was determined
by my own struggles,
and how much was determined by your inability
to accept it.
I was scared of the way I loved.
You were scared of being loved.

I laughed as you attempted to explain to me
how you thought we were soulmates,
while avoiding the use of those words.
If I hadn't believed it too,
I don't think I would have had any idea
what you were trying to say.
    - *I'm glad that I did.*

I always thought the love of my life
would be a romantic one.
But for me,
    it was you.

The way you looked at me while I was laughing,
like I really was the whole sun,
breathing beams of golden light into your world.
It was real.
This was real.

I didn't even know I was capable of loving like that.

Until I loved you.

I wish I had written more
in this period of our story.
But, it's almost more meaningful now that I didn't.
There simply aren't enough words
in this language
to accurately invoke
what it was like
to love
and be loved
by you.

Just for a second,
I submerged into divinity
within the love I held for you.
Maybe that is why you were so hard to lose.

One day I woke up to realize,
somewhere along the way,
you became my best friend.
My favorite person to walk this planet with.
And the same thing happened
the day I woke up to realize that
that title no longer suited you.

On your shoulders I have placed
all of my truest beliefs.
Invisible wings that I hoped
with enough faith,
could bring you back to me.
Because some people are just meant to stay,
and love conquers all.
Right?

THE BEGINNING OF THE END

I throw myself so deeply
into the things that I love,
that they swallow me whole.
At first,
I thrive on it.
The exploration of the caves I've created.
Until the walls begin to collapse,
and I find myself trapped.
Unable to bring air into my lungs.
Confused how my inspiration
became desperation.

Love isn't sacrifice,
but it is compromise.
Love is putting someone else first,
when you find that in this moment
they need you.
Putting something of yours to the side,
knowing that for this brief moment
your love is stronger than your pain.
Knowing that getting to be there in this vulnerability
is a gift.

      - The belief that made me doubt you.

I love you so much that
I will take a love that feels black.
A love that turns me gray
when I was once a sunny day.
    - I thought you were the reason I was happy.

It's hard to look at a relationship you once loved,
and feel exhausted by it now.
It's hard not to wonder what,
or who, changed.
It's okay if it was you.
You do not owe yourself to anyone or anything.
Change happens.
Change is okay.

> *- But you can't decide who leaves and who stays.*

When I am hurting,
I tend to tap into my love
for other people.
Let it warm me,
when my heart forgets
how to love me.

I can't remember the last time I truly laughed with her. The last time we connected and laughed together. I remember sharing that room in that house in St. Louis. We laid in each of our beds after a twelve hour drive of sitting next to each other. We had turned off the lights, having just the street lights leaking in from behind the blinds. Listening to country night sounds playing off of your phone. I rolled over to face you and found you facing me. And I just lit up from the inside out. An uncontrollable smile spread across my face. I remember thinking just how grateful I am to have this person in my life. To love this person so deeply, that I could feel my heart basking in a golden light. To feel so deeply intertwined with this person. To hold a love for this person that felt purer than anything I have ever felt. Just looking at her and feeling comfort and love. I can still feel myself in that moment now. That is one of my most treasured memories that I carry with me on this earth.

That night was almost one year ago. So, what happened since that moment that I don't feel that connection anymore? I think that camping trip this past summer was a turning point. But if I'm being honest, there were things leading up to it. Like when you went vegan. God, I was so proud of you. Your heart has all the capacity to love and love. Love this planet. Love these animals. Love yourself. To do the hard thing, when it was going to be so good for you. But then you told me about how your family thought you were doing it for me. And I began to worry if that was true. But you spoke from your heart when you said this decision made you feel good. And that is all I ever wanted for you.

Then you went back on it. And you looked at abuse like it was nothing new. You stopped believing in yourself and maybe my confidence began to waiver too.

I don't remember how I felt exactly on your birthday. I think I still felt pretty close to you that day. But uncomfortable with the new dynamic. There being more than just you and me. You started doing more with her and she began to show up in situations that were once just you and I.

Oh, that day when we were switching around your apartment. I made a face and a silly noise at one of your cousins and you looked at me and said, "Your future husband is in for a real treat." How I wish for a day like that.

But, remember when (I don't remember the date) but we were talking on the phone, and you told me how your aunt had called me your girlfriend? A part of me had been worrying that you maybe you loved me a little too much. I never ever wanted to hurt you.

Then came the camping trip with all of my friends. Your aunt had told you that I brought you with me to pitch my tent. And then my sister called you, "my bitch." But you had every reason to be there. You deserved to be there. And I wanted you there because I adore your company.

But, when I'm honest, I always had hidden insecurities that I didn't deserve your love. I felt guilty. And this just let it all out. I always had this fear that I was not being a good enough friend. You deserve everything in this world and more.

And then we had the business. I don't know that I believe we were meant to be business partners, you're a do-er and I'm a planner. Planning helped me cope. Researching and having something to think about helped me cope. At this point my mind was playing tricks on me, and I was desperate for an escape. You began to ask me about business stuff and want me to do business stuff, not knowing how difficult it was for me. I barely knew either. Not until the water had already filled my lungs. You expected me to do. I expected you to plan. I would have much rather just had my best friend.

I'm pretty sure I've told you before, but you made me feel seen in a way no one else on this planet ever has. I think I stopped feeling seen when you didn't recognize how much I was struggling. It all just went downhill from there. I've been killing myself, trying to recognize the stranger beside me. Forcing myself to stand next to you as I felt like a burden.

BETRAYAL

(Am I enough?)

I guess the truth will always come out.
I just never expected it would be you,
who would take my heartache
and turn it into your own.

I don't know how to tell you,
but I know how to write.
So I'm going to write and write
until whatever words I am hiding come out.
Because every time I think of telling you,
I forget them myself.

First and foremost, I have nothing but love in my heart for you. But I have all of these feelings that I am trying to come to terms with too. Though these feelings are not directed towards you, many of them have risen due to you and our relationship.

I am still so immensely hurt and feel deeply betrayed. You broke my trust and I am trying to deal, and forgive, and give it time to heal. But I don't feel ready. There is still poison in my veins. I gave you my time and energy to understand every place you are coming from. To understand what it was that was bothering you. But I don't feel like that time was returned.

Because I told you how much I'm hurting. I told you why. I told you not all of my hurt was about you. But you are still talking about everyone else like everything is fine and I want nothing to do with them right now. I don't feel fine. And if you had heard me at all, if you cared at all, you would not keep talking about them like everything is okay.

Relationships of all kinds need work. And I am really trying to put in the work. I am working on myself, and on trying to better understand you and give you what you need.

Where is that for me? Maybe I'm asking for too much. Because you tell me you hear me. That you're not invalidating me. That you're here, if I want to talk. But I'm having a hard time believing it. Because I talked and I talked, and I still don't feel like you listened.

Maybe I've changed. Maybe I want more than you can give. Every once in a while, I feel okay. But then you say something that sends me back, and I feel the dagger in my heart.

I guess I don't know what you want from me anymore. Because I stand here, and I give and I give. But I don't even know you anymore. I don't know me standing next to you.

You text me and text me again about something that has nothing to do with you. That feels like gossip to me. Then have all these feelings when I don't respond? What is it that you want from me? My energy? My time? To engage in seemingly meaningless conversations and feed your fuel?

This is beginning to sound like something I've seen before. Roads I've already walked. But this time, I don't feel as if I'm being manipulated to stay. Because I want to heal your hurt. I want to know you. I want to stand beside you and understand. I want to be with you and laugh with you. But I can't keep putting what I'm feeling aside to do it. I don't want to walk away, and I don't want you to either. But if I've learned anything at all, if we keep walking on this track, the train is going to come and everything I'm avoiding will knock the wind straight out.

I genuinely believe that some part of you was trying to make me feel better. But it was like you said those things so that you could say something hurtful next.

> *I would take a bullet for you...*
> *I betrayed you because I was hurt...*
> *Every memory I have is of you...*

As if to disguise the ugly. I don't want a mask. I don't want a disguise.

> *I'm sorry, but...*
> *I'm telling you the truth; the truth just hurts.*
> *You're selfish, you're trying to look innocent.*

Shoving things down my throat to keep the bile down. Not once did you say you were wrong and not ask me for an apology. Instead you gave me, "I'm sorry," and still threw swords at me. Your apologies felt disingenuous. And if that is the case, as I believe, then tell me.

Because even through my pain, every sorry I said I meant. It didn't need a but. It didn't need an excuse. Since that day, I have been analyzing every move you make and I know I have. I don't want to be. I want to be able to forgive you. But I'm still stuck. Because every analysis comes back positive. Every time I reach out I am finding something I didn't want to. That I bled all that I had to bleed out, and I am still trying so damn hard. I still don't feel heard. I don't feel seen. I don't feel cared for.

Notice how never once I called you names? Never once did I make excuses for you? It's because I can speak my truth with compassion. It's because I can tell you how I feel while still having consideration for you. It is because I care about you. I'm not going to take the poison in me and try to give it to you. I just want you to see it and understand it. I don't even mind if you can't heal it. How you react to it, that is all yours. But it tells me a lot.

If you knew me at all, If you saw me at all, you wouldn't have called me selfish. You would have known that I don't have a selfish bone in my body. That I will burn and burn, to get EVERYONE out of the fire. That *that*, is my hamartia. You would have known that that hurts even more than the original wound.

What was your intention going into the conversation we had? Mine was to heal both of us, to get us both out. Heal our relationship and see what it can be now. It felt like all you wanted was for me to understand you. To fix you. To cater towards you. And this doesn't feel okay to me. Where is the give and take? Where is the desire to grow? Where is the desire to rebuild that solid energizing relationship again?

Again, I ask, what do you want from me? To be what you need? To give and give and give? Just to sit down and shut up? You want something from me that you could get anywhere. I'm really working on knowing and feeling my worth. And I am worth more than just a body beside you. I am an incredible human being, I don't need you to tell me. But I shouldn't have to sit here and convince you either. I am worth more than the way I was treated. I deserve better. And trying to salvage that with anyone else is not worth my energy. The relationship you and I share is so special. I love spending time with you. The connection, laughter, joy, and time we share was once so special. I love spending time with you, because you are *you*.

So maybe we are on different pages. That I can understand. Maybe we express ourselves in different ways. But I cannot sacrifice my peace anymore, pretending that this is okay with me. I am willing to find a new page. Ready for a new chapter. But it's like you just want me to flip through the book, until I can find you on whatever page you refuse to leave. I can't do this. It hurts so much that I can't. Because I'm afraid of losing you. But I'm not at peace in our friendship anymore. I am drained more than I am energized. Hurting more than I am healing. Our relationship doesn't feel like it's growing in the way that it needs.

To the moon and back,
Abigail

You were more committed
to misunderstanding me,
and to defending your truth,
that was never under attack,
than you were committed
to working through this together.
It was as if my hurt,
felt like a personal betrayal to you.
Why else would you try so hard to justify yourself?

I kept trying to help you understand,
but you just got mad.
Leaving every time
I brought it up again.

No matter the pain I am in,
I still try to justify the reasons that you were cruel.
Even when you set me on fire,
I still make excuses
just to drive the scars in deeper.
Because for you to hurt me like that,
you must have been hurting even worse.
Right?

PRETENDING
(That this is enough.)

I felt like I was sitting next to a stranger.
She sat there talking to me,
and I sat there lifeless.
Drowning on her words,
ready to burst into tears over the excused
and explained betrayal
I was supposed to get over.
I could tell how her mood changed
when she was around me.
Like I was poisoning the air
we were both breathing.
It's like I've forgotten how to exist…

How the hell does someone forget how to exist?

When I granted you permission
to my written thoughts and experiences,
you took it upon yourself to accept that
as a burden,
and not a privilege.

      - Proving my story.

Destruction.
That is my biggest fear.
That like Medusa,
I can harm people with just one look.
That everyone I love is Icarus
and I am the sun.
That just like the stars,
with too much excitement,
I will spontaneously combust.
That you are the forest,
and I am the lit cigarette.
That I am the bomb,
and your beautiful inspiration is a match.
That I am destruction.

I am so scared to lose you,
but just as scared to love you.

Maybe I didn't want to be the sun or the moon,
knowing they would always change.
Instead,
I became a star,
because they seem to stay the same.
The price of this kind of stability is understanding,
one day I would fall.
And I would not be full again.
I would not rise tomorrow.
I would take comfort in the knowledge
that I'd never have to worry
about how I would relight.
Because shooting stars are permissed
to go down in a blaze.
They inspire wishes to be made
in their dying breath.
There is magic in stars,
within something so inevitable as death.
No one expects shooting stars to come back.

My heart does not know how to beat
if no one sees it.
        - Codependency.

I feel guilty when someone is taking care of me.
Shameful that the role is not reversed.
Worried about what could happen
when their touch is not all healing.
I was always too much,
because your touch wasn't enough.

    - I didn't want you to fix me.

Every word I spoke prefaced with,
"I'm not trying to…"
I was always sorry,
before I even started.

      - I can't keep feeling sorry for me.

I let people keep tearing me apart,
and I think half of it is that
I'm scared they will turn away
if I stand up for myself.
That I'm not worth more than this
em0tional abus3.
That they wouldn't need me
if I didn't act as a punching bag.
That my purpose is to be a sponge,
and if I fail that purpose...
I won't be worth loving anymore.

     - Call it what it is.

The discomfort comes about
with the fear
that I might abandon myself.
The fear that I will give more
than what I want to give,
in order to fill someone else's cup.
  - You don't have to be swallowed in order to express
    your love.

You are my person. There is not a day I will spend on this planet in which that will not be true. This is a relationship that I'm not prepared to walk away from, ever. I'm not in a place where I can put this relationship first. There are things here that are hurting me. There are things here that are hurting you. I am immensely grateful for the lessons and growing I've been able to learn and do. And I cannot reduce this to a lesson.

I am simultaneously anxious and crushed every time my phone rings. I am tired of asking people to see me, to hear me, to show me their love. I am trying so hard to be what I want to be. I am giving so much energy to myself right now. I am experiencing a million different lessons at once. Trying to figure out my balance. It's hard. Every day is hard. And I need the close relationships around me to be my breath of fresh air. I need them to be vulnerable and open. I need to be able to trust. I need to be energized by the people around me more than I'm drained. And here, in this space, I'm being drained.

I'm self-conscious of every move I make, and I don't trust you anymore. It's partly who I am and partly the situation itself. I feel like I'm the one moving all the chess pieces on the board, and when I move them wrong you just stop watching the game. But half the pieces should be yours. I'm holding all of these things that aren't mine to hold and I don't want to anymore. I'm terrified of what happens if I put them down. I can't fit myself into a box for other people anymore and here it feels like I still am. It confuses me to no end how next to you I can have the most genuine moments, and the most disingenuous too.

I keep making excuses. I'm hurting, but I've done some hurting too. Therefore, my needs are irrelevant. I'm punishing myself for being human. I'm letting myself be taken advantage of. As if pain is what I deserve. I know my worth and I'm worth more than this. I love myself enough to know where I set my bar. I deserve honesty, love, trust, to be cheered on, a life vest when

I'm floating out to sea, forgiveness, and for my feelings to be cared for. With all of my light, comes all of my dark. Tell me it does not make you uncomfortable.

To the moon and back,
Abigail

I figured out what was hurting me so bad.
I never got to grieve a relationship
that fell apart
without permission.
Always blaming myself,
and wondering what it was that broke.
Thinking I must be getting what I deserve.
Not letting myself feel
because my pain isn't justified,
if I didn't ask for it.
But my person no longer sees me as theirs.
And now I know...
The jealousy.
The anger.
They were hiding the grief
I didn't want to accept.

    - Losing control.

You couldn't keep, *living in the past.*
You were, *just ready to move on.*
And, *hoped I could respect that.*
You spoke my language so well,
that I agreed with you.
And I tried with everything that I was
to respect something
that never deserved it.

I'm beginning to realize
that although I understand
why you did the things you did,
that it still isn't excusable behavior.
It was still a mistake.
That I can understand you,
but I also must respect me
and what it is that I need.

> - I didn't need you to tell me why you did it, I needed
> you to tell me you were sorry and mean it.

I didn't know what "emotionally unavailable" really meant,
until I needed you.
Until I sobbed at your feet
and begged you to love me
the way that I wanted you to.
And you simply couldn't.

You shoved words down my throat
to distract me from the bile
that rose as I stood next to you.
I choked on those words,
then tucked them into my heart.
Never listening to the pit in my stomach
pleading at me to run.
Instead, I let you force blame on me
and thought my own body
was agreeing with you.
That I was wrong.
That I wasn't worthy.
That I wasn't enough.

Turns out, I never lost myself at all.
I just didn't know how to translate.

This was the end,
we both knew it.
You watched me break with an apathetic stare.
Eyes glazed over,
I didn't recognize this monster.
My silence was deafening,
but my tears too much.

ABANDONMENT

(Are you enough?)

To my best friend, my person,

I think I've only had a few moments in this life that have absolutely crushed my soul. Only a few moments that have actually broken my heart. Only a few moments in which I've been living so hard, that my heart could actually be broken. I'm sure you can guess the others. But that's not actually what I want to talk about.

The funny thing is, I wouldn't call my broken hearts the worst moments of my life. No... the worst periods of time had nothing to do with the moment my heart broke. I guess at this point I'm just rambling. I don't even know where to start. It's a battle between the grief, the love, and the fire in my heart.

It's so hard to let the fire come out. I don't want it to burn the love. The love is more than the grief. Because even in the moments where my heart stops beating, freezing in a moment of pain, I still feel love for you. I'm still so proud of you. I still feel so grateful to walk this life in your presence. Watching you grow, and learn, and hearing you talk. You are my favorite book.

The fire wants to say that this isn't fair. The fire wants to hate you. The fire is in a rage of guilt and shame and injustice. The fire cannot believe we let ourselves trust you. Let you in... just like you asked. I can't believe I almost trusted you when you said you would be here beside me. I almost trusted you when you said you loved me. I justified every action you've ever taken that caused me pain. Always in shame. That I expected too much. That I was too needy. But I realize now, that had someone come to me with their deepest insecurities, their deepest fears, tear filled eyes... I would have met them with nothing but compassion. We are allowed to have insecurities. We are allowed to have things we need. We are allowed to need a specific language to understand. I was there every day. When you came to me in need I was always there. I didn't ask you to be something else. I took everything you have ever said to heart and sat next to you when words seemed too hard. I tried to give you all of the love I have in my body. Even in the moments I didn't know what to say, I did my best to let you know that I love you with everything I have. That whatever storm you are facing, I will be there next to you. I gave everything I could possibly give.

But you could not give me the same. All I needed was to know that I was safe with you. That you were there to support me in whatever it was, and that you loved me unconditionally. Just the other day I told my therapist that you were the only person I've ever experienced unconditional love with... and now I feel so stupid for ever even thinking that. You are a coward. You cannot handle unconditional.

It is not always my responsibility to fit into a place too small. How can I tell exactly what I am feeling, when I can't even feel your love? I tried every day to cater to your feelings. Every day, to make sure that I showed you how much I love you. Every day, to make up for what happened. And in my moments of weakness, you cannot handle it. I NEEDED YOU. I NEEDED MY BEST FRIEND. I NEEDED YOU ON MY BIRTHDAY. I NEEDED YOU WHEN I DIDN'T HAVE THE STRENGTH TO LIVE ANOTHER DAY. I NEEDED TO KNOW THAT I HAD SOMEONE THAT LOVED ME. I NEEDED TO FEEL THAT LOVE. YOU TALK ABOUT ME SHUTTING DOWN. YOU ARE JUST AS MUCH A COWARD AS I. I NEED YOU FOR CHRIST-MAS. YOU ARE THE ONLY PERSON ON THIS EARTH THAT I WANT BESIDE ME WHEN MY HEART CAN'T TAKE ANYTHING ELSE.

EVEN WHEN I WASN'T HERE, I STILL FOUND THE STRENGTH TO BE THERE FOR YOU. EVEN WHEN I COULDN'T TELL IF YOU WANTED IT. EVEN WHEN I WAS A BLEEDING HEART. THE MINUTE YOU WERE STRUG-GLING. THE MINUTE I FELT YOU PULLING AWAY.

I guess part of it was me knowing you were about to leave. I grabbed on with everything I could. I tried everything I could think of. Nothing was enough.

You really picked the best time to leave. Right when the depression was pulling back under. Right after I gave you what you said you wanted and exposed myself in a way that I've never shown anyone. Right when I was finally letting myself be loved. Right when I was working on building up my worth. Building up my confidence that I am worth loving, just as I am. Just as I was learning to trust someone I love with all the things I've never ensured anyone with.

This fucking crushed me. I always had to be the one to reach out. Always had to be the one to apologize. Always had to be the one to talk us through every situation. How naive of me to believe I could trust you. How naive of me to believe you would someday love me in a way I could understand. That someday you would show me you care. How naive of me to believe you would stay. How naive of me to believe I could be your favorite book… When you have never liked reading.

I fear what happens next. I am scared you are gone for good. I am scared you don't love me anymore. I am scared of what happens if you do. I'm scared that you still won't be able to love and support me in the way that I need. I am scared you are okay with abandoning me. I am scared of the waiting. I am scared of what you'll say. I'm scared of what I'll say.

I'm torn apart by the idea that I might not hear your voice on Christmas. I'm torn apart by why it is you decided you needed to leave. I'm torn apart that I have expressed what a trigger abandonment is for me, and you couldn't have the courtesy to tell me if you were coming back, even if you didn't know when.

I am absolutely broken by the idea that this could be it. That I could lose you forever. God, I cannot imagine that. I don't even remember the last time I hugged you. The last time I felt connected to you by something other than animosity. I can't believe that there is a chance you will not love me anymore.

My goodness. I do not know what to do with this bleeding heart. I hope you are okay. I hope you know how much I love you. I hope in your space you confer with the stars and discover whatever it is that you are looking for. I hope that you are not so thirsty that you begin to drink from poisoned hearts. I love you, in this life and everyone before and after, into infinity.

To the moon and back,
Abigail

I keep compulsively reaching for my phone.
Wanting to send something.
Ask a question.
Beg you to talk.
Tell you I love you.
That I'm sorry.
And then I remember,
I promised I wouldn't.

Part of me is prepared to lose everyone.
Part of me prepares the minute we meet.
I finally trusted...
just enough,
that I wasn't prepared to lose you too.

It hurts that you had to leave to work through this.
Even if you didn't want to work through it together,
why was it you couldn't work on it beside me?
Why couldn't you just have taken an ounce of accountability?
You retaliated over the pain that my being distant
while I was exhausted caused you,
before ever even telling me it was hurting you.
How in the hell does my depression, excuse your actions?
Did you do this to get even?
When I tried to get close to you again, you said it *scared you*.
What did you want from me?
Was it me, who was too intense?
Or the feelings you felt when I was around?
Why couldn't you make up your mind?
Did you shut off from me?
Or the world?
Did it hurt you to leave?

    - Answers I may never get.

Five.
That is the number of days I can go
before the urge to reach out
consumes me,
and I reach for the phone.
I wish I could meticulously calculate you
out of my head for good.
Make a list of the things to do today:
Not text you.
Not care what you're doing.
Not check your page or look for the last post you liked.
Set a goal for the days I want to be able to go
without hearing from you,
and still be okay.
And just as I think that I'm strong enough to push the urge
one more day...
I remember.
There is no goal I actually want to obtain.
Because one day without you
is too many.
And I resent every day,
every person,
every being,
that gets to know you when I don't.
I resent all of this time that I'm missing.

Sometimes the missing you
makes me forget—
there are so many things still left to love.
Because I wish so deeply,
you would let one of them be you.

Do you love me?
Or do you love that I love you?

When I asked you to love me,
it seemed that you couldn't.
But before any of that,
you drew portraits of me
and took an endless number of photos whenever I asked.
Saved me as your screensaver
and always knew how to make me laugh and laugh.
You made me feel loved in ways
I wouldn't have even known to ask for.
I'm scared of becoming addicted to this affection again.
Maybe that's why I pushed you away with requests for more.
But then again,
at just one criticism,
you stopped loving me like that.

You had a sick way
of withholding affection
whenever I wasn't exactly
what you wanted me to be.

You set me up for this.
Illuminating my room in pink in your absence
with the simple reminder that you love me.
Weaving yourself into every thread of my existence.
It's as if your fingers grazed everything I've ever known,
and now it all glows with a hue just for you.
You spoke of a future we would never get,
but took mine anyways.
You may be gone,
but now I see you everywhere I look.
Why did you love me like that
if you were just going to rip it all away?
YOU DID THIS TO ME.
IT WASN'T ME WHO YOU WERE RUNNING FROM.

You're right.
I am *fucking angry.*
Because you took my favorite thing,
and destroyed it.
I should have listened
when you said
if you wanted to tell me,
you would have.
When you wanted me to stop asking.
Or when you wanted me to anticipate
the right questions to ask,
and when.
I should have listened.
I should have left first.

God dammit.
Tell me to leave you alone
or something.
Give me a reason to hate you.
Give me a darkened picture so that I never want to think of you
again.
　　　- Be careful what you wish for.

Oh, so now you want to ignore me?
Watch this.
Let's see how you ignore me now.
　　　- Setting fires in your name.

I screamed.
Oh, how I screamed.
I let that grief tear through me so deeply
it ripped the earth beneath my feet.
      - This is where I fell in.

As flames crept in,
you took off running.
Righteously proclaiming you were,
setting me free.
As if I was some caged-up animal
whose best chance was open gates.

      - You chose this. I would have left if I had wanted to.

Grieving a loss that wasn't due to death
is like
loving someone that never existed.
There is no funeral.
No acceptable period to grieve.
No baked goods,
or flowers,
or people to surround you while you cry.
And every time I see you,
I break again.
     And again.
          And again.

I feel frozen.
I don't want time to move on without her.
If you miss someone,
was it their time to leave?
Shouldn't it feel complete,
if they weren't meant to be?
Missing them...
It just feels unfinished.

If you loved me like you said you did,
you would have never left.

- Honey, she was always going to leave. This was never about you.

I felt most like myself with you…
I didn't just lose you,
I lost me too.

Here it is. This is the final letter.
No not a suicide note.
But it is a goodbye.

I miss you… a lot. I don't feel connected to you at all, and it hurts. You are my best friend. You are my person. And I honestly believe at one point I was yours. But I don't think that this is true anymore. That's okay. Obviously, we are on two separate pages. I have found that my anger and jealousy are coming from a place of grief. I have been trying too hard to be something that I'm not. Trying to make myself loveable to you. I am okay with making compromises, but I'm overcompensating. I have been holding things that are not mine to carry and it is squashing who I am. Because naturally, I am inquisitive, I am emotional, I need clear communication and I am a caretaker. I like to show my love in a multitude of ways, and I love all of this about me. I am worthy of love and support no matter the state I am in. Someday they'll say I had a heart of pure gold, and a soul on fire.

I don't understand why loving and supporting me makes you feel like you're not supporting yourself. But that is a problem that doesn't pertain to me. We can talk about it and explore it together, if you would like. But my close relationships should be supportive the majority of the time. I really don't think that that is too much to ask for.

My love for you is unconditional. No matter what, I will always be there to support and love you and I think I have shown that in a million ways. I don't feel that from you. When I am feeling weak or upset, 90% of the time you aren't there. You get defensive and take things personally.

I want to work through this with you. Everything seems like a fight, but to me I'm just trying to talk and work it out. I don't want to carry this anymore. I'm having a really hard time moving forward and still missing you. I know this is how you deal with things. But it's not me. I can't hear about the person that has taken my spot in your life and not feel hurt. I can't hide all of my hurt. It's turning me cold and angry and that's not who I am. I love you with all of my heart and I need time to grieve. Because I do feel like I've lost something so important and meaningful in my life. Going forward I'm not going to hide it anymore, and I anticipate anger from you. This is my honest and authentic self and I refuse to make myself anything else. If you're not ready for it, I understand. I'm going to heal either way. But, I'm not going to subject myself to things that make me feel bad about me or my emotions anymore.

To the moon and back,
Abigail

I have this huge fear of people leaving
when I tell them something that hurts me.
Something in me has been conditioned,
that once I share my feelings,
they will be taken
in a way I didn't mean them.
And I will be abandoned,
and left to deal with the guilt
of chasing them away.
        - I didn't mean to hurt you.

I have this huge fear of people leaving
when I tell them something that hurts me.
Something in me has been conditioned,
that once I share my feelings,
they will be taken
in a way I didn't mean them.
And I will be abandoned,
and left to deal with the guilt
of chasing them away.

> - You ran away and you don't get to take my emotions
> with you.

RETURN
(Are we enough?)

Everything we had went up in flames.
And now that you've come back...
Are you asking to rebuild?
Did you grieve?
Or are you still wandering through the ash,
looking for old picture frames?

I know I said I was done.
But then you came back.
What do I do with that?

I have not one clue where to start. Not one clue how this is supposed to go. But maybe that's just it. Maybe I'm not supposed to worry about everything else right now. Not worry about you, or how to fix us. Do I even know how to do that? Because even now, I wanted to replace the word, "us" with something else... but no word seems right. Everything I did somehow became wrong. It's going to take me a while to become me again in front of you. I don't know how to trust you. But I'm willing to try.

Sometimes my hope feels poisonous, even to me. A hope so massive it becomes painful. But it's the one thing I always have. It's something I can trust and build from. So let's start there.

When I'm being completely honest, I don't feel any hope around being close to you again. There is nothing to hope for. I can't see the future. And everything that once existed feels completely gone, and I don't miss it. We didn't leave on good terms or gently. We left in an explosion and every flower in a garden that I loved was gone. Before you left, you took everything light and twisted it to dark. I don't know how to tell you that I don't feel the same, that I don't miss you. I look at you, and I don't know who I'm looking at. I don't know which side of you I'm going to get. The girl laughing beside me in the car. The girl who I could talk about everything under the sky with. The girl who wanted to save money to live in a house with me. Or the girl who holds everything in her eyes instead of letting the words spill out of her mouth. The girl I can't trust apologies from because she will negate them months later. The girl that could talk about a future with me, but didn't want to hear the same words if they came from my mouth. I can't remember the last time I looked at you, and saw my best friend looking back. Her, I do miss.

It's hard for me to understand. Every side of my ugly points straight back within. But every side of yours pointed straight at me. Everything that I said and did became hurtful to you. Everything that I enjoyed, that made me *me*, you didn't like. After the first betrayal, you negated every experience we had ever had. Everything that I once loved, became a lie. You didn't just shut me out. You burned every picture in the whole damn house.

And my god do I get it. I can't help but get it. Empathy and hope both seem like such kind words, but can't I just get a moment in which the only person I think about is me? Can I stop making excuses for everyone else? Can I stop making excuses for you?

I know that you feel guilty. I know why. I'm not saying that you're not right to feel that way. But I am saying that you don't have to feel guilty. You feeling guilty about it, doesn't do anything for either one of us. I get needing patience, and it's something I am willing to give. Here is the million dollar question: Why is it that you feel guilty? Because honestly, I don't think that the things you feel guilty for, are the things that hurt me most.

And hurt it did. Reopening it now, it still hurts. I was fine. I was okay. I grieved and I let go and I forgave myself. I did everything I was supposed to do. I have no faith that putting myself in a vulnerable position in front of you again is safe to do. I have no faith that you enjoy being around the person that I am. I have little faith that I can exist around you without censoring myself, at least not without serious effort. I have no faith that I can say all of this to you and that you won't get defensive. That you won't throw out something that I did that hurt you too.

What I do know, is that I'm not going to let it get to be like that again. I may have a patience that could move mountains, but I am worth more than I was once treated. I am a fucking gem.

I have little faith that my new boundaries aren't going to send you running. I guess what I'm trying to say is, it's going to take some time to trust you again. I'm going to need reason to trust you again. But I am willing to try.

To the moon and back,
Abigail

You didn't destroy us.
You couldn't have even if you tried.
Broke my heart,
yes.
But would I let you do it again...
Also yes.
We were fated.
I know it with every ounce of courage
in my veins.
We are soulmates,
and there isn't anything we can do about it,
except give in.

The thing I can count on most,
is the fact that you will let me mourn you,
just to come back from the dead.
        - A fresh start is supposed to be mutual.

I don't know how to say this,
but I'm going to try.
Because I love you
and I know you love me too.

It is not easy, having you waltz back into my life. My mind. My heart. I was actually beginning to feel better. I was at a place where I was going to be okay, without you. Seeing you and hearing you speak, it broke the stone that was encasing my heart. Rivers of sorrow, pain, remorse, anger, love, and disgust, all came pouring out. Because it wasn't like you just shut me out. You didn't just slam the door in my face. You burnt down the whole damn house.

I still don't know exactly what to say. I think I will try separating all the feelings. Analyzing them one by one...

Hey, look at that. I still don't know what to say. I keep trying to pick one. The easiest... or the nicest... the one that won't hurt. But they all hurt. I'm scared to hurt you. I'm scared to lose you all over again.

Ah, fear. Cute.

I'm scared to feel hurt again too. I'm scared of my own capacity for suffering. Recently, I've learned that our emotions are a rubber band. You can stretch into joy, but not without stretching into sorrow. And the greater you stretch into despair or depression or grief, the greater you'll be able slingshot over into love, inspiration, the feeling of being alive.

So here I sit, wondering how far my rubber band stretched when I was around you. How far into the positive infinity did it have to go, to snap back and break my heart as intensely as it did. You were, are, my soulmate. I know that straight into my bones. Could that be why it hurt so bad?

Sunshine, god dammit. You are my soulmate and you tore my heart straight out of my chest and I love you and I miss you and I want to talk to you and I want to be around you, but I also know that for some reason I can't. And I could go on for days with all of my theories and thoughts for why this is the case.

I'm scared that you only love a version of me when I exist as so many more than one. I'm scared that even if you think you want to be around me, it's only certain "me's". I'm scared that you will think it's true when you tell me that this isn't the case, but one day you will learn that it isn't, and I'll end up watching you break again and think that it's because of me. I'm scared that my heart can't take another heartbreak. I'm scared that I think I have a love bigger than this world, a forgiveness that can conquer all, but someday I'll learn that I don't.

I'm scared that I'm too much. I'm scared that my love isn't enough. I'm scared that I'll think everything is okay, because you say so, even when truthfully I know it isn't, and then one day you'll turn around and say I was right all along. I'm scared that I'll end up in old patterns. I'm scared that I won't stay true to myself. I'm scared that I won't be able to love you anymore the way that I did. I'm scared that you won't say what you want to. I'm scared I'll carry too much. I'm scared that I'll choose the wrong road in the yellow wood and I'll never be able to go back. I'm scared all you see when you look at me are my biggest moments of weakness. Because you did. You saw them all. And you couldn't handle it.

I'm angry because if you couldn't handle me then, why the fuck do you think you get to show up now? I'm ashamed because when I look at you I see every one of my ugliest moments. I see a girl that I don't want to be. I'm ashamed of the pain I put you through. And add that to the list, because I feel guilty for feeling ashamed. Here I am, trying to feel out your pain. Wanting to heal you. Again.

I'm scared that I can't be what you want me to be. I'm scared that I'll try. I'm scared that you'll leave. I'm scared that I won't be able to tear down the walls that my heart put up. Because without her, I can't be anything.

I know you were hurting then, and you're still hurting

now. I am not healed enough to step back into a house of shattered windows and start cleaning up. I want to. Every muscle in my body wants to. I want to clean, and fix. And I know that this isn't what I should do. That it wouldn't be good for either one of us. And I know I shouldn't make assumptions, but looking at you now, it sure seems like you still don't want to even touch the thought of healing yourself. Tell me, *how do you expect to heal us?*

You never did explain why you continued to decide that I was treating you like a significant other. Don't think I didn't notice the word and reference to, "us," in the apology you typed out. It was of utter surprise that you used a word like that. When once the word, "relationship," sent you over the edge.

I think I need you to prepare me before you tell me all of your hurt. In everyday conversation you tell me so much of the ugly, and it's just feels like a lot sometimes. I can tell you trust me, and I love that. I just need you to ask first, if it's okay, because otherwise it feels like all of my energy is being drained.

And I feel like we need to talk about her. Really, just whether or not you still think I was/am jealous. I just want to clarify all the thoughts. I was hurt because I knew when you were leaving. I could feel you pulling away before you completely did. And I was watching you replace me with someone else. Then you would cancel our plans without telling me, or go do something that I had wanted to do too, but with her. All of these things seemed little, even to me. But it turns out they meant more than I knew, because my heart crumpled, watching someone else become your person.

I'm scared to tell you I love you. Because the kinder my words got, the sharper the knife on your tongue became. The colder your heart grew. I am scared to feel love for someone that I don't feel like I can express my love for.

Then touch became so weird. You wouldn't sit next to me, or anywhere near me. Honestly, there came a point in time when it seemed like every part of me disgusted you. Emotionally, Mentally, Physically. I watched you seemingly grow to hate me, and at this point, I began to disgust myself too. For years I watched myself through your eyes and felt more love than I had ever known. Then in a span of weeks, those eyes that I trusted left me knowing the deepest hatred too.

I'm scared to cry in front of you. I'm scared that you'll think it's manipulation. I'm scared that it'll make you upset. I'm scared that you'll say things you don't mean. I'm scared that it hurts you every time I accuse you of lying. I'm scared that I won't be able to stop. I'm scared that you won't be able to take any of this in, because you are drifted too far from yourself.

I'm scared that I was a shitty friend. I'm scared that I'm still not enough. I'm scared of everything that I'm feeling. I'm scared that it's all too much. I'm scared to be sad in front of you again. For months, all I wanted to let you see was me thriving. I wanted to make you watch just how well I was doing. I didn't want you to see the vulnerability you took advantage of. I didn't want to show you just how much losing you hurt me. I wanted to make sure the last pictures of me in your mind were not of the sad girl, but of a shining sun.

This may not be the cleanest letter I've ever written, but I can tell you that I feel better. My heart is pumping again. So, thank you for that.

To the moon and back,
Abigail

Whether it is unwillingness or inability,
it is sad,
the way you cannot see my truth.

You're so unreliable.
But *damn,*
you are predictable.

You told obscenely bold lies
and I knew it.
But when you swore it was the truth,
how could I be right?
  - I really wanted to believe you.

I can't meet you in the mundane,
and you can't meet me in the extraordinary.
I'm not sure what to do with that.

Every time my phone rings,
I still hope that it's you.
And I still feel my stomach tie in knots
when it's not your name that comes through.
Every time the doorbell rings,
my stomach does the same thing.
Funny… it kind of feels like anxiety.

Because you know where I stand,
and it will always be right here.
I couldn't leave even if I wanted to.
My love for you is so overwhelmingly consuming,
that I don't want to leave.
Instead, I take excuse after excuse
and let you put everyone else first.
I beg you to pick me up
like a broken old toy,
playing a distorted yet familiar sound
from a box somewhere under your bed,
reminding you,
I was once yours.
You dig me out and
for that moment,
I become your personal shining star.
Illuminating every memory I hold for you.
But, when you're done
and tired
or bored
or ready to leave because
I am *too much,*
I lay back down,
lingering in the place that you left me,
yearning for the day
you'll remember that you love me.

> - Someday, my love for me will swallow the love I have
> for you. Someday, I'll stop waiting for you.

The final letter part 2.
Because I think this might finally be it.
I think the storm might actually be over.

I'm laying my weapons down and saying I'm sorry. I let my ego get the best of me and I didn't see it until now. You showed up and apologized and said all the right things and I looked for cracks, scared to forgive you. I inadvertently tested if you were going to leave again, by poking you until you did. I put on a show, not wanting you to see the pain you put me through, hurting you instead. You hurt me, I set fires and hide. I hurt you, you throw swords and leave. Too proud to come find each other. I'm here because I'm confident now that this is our lesson. Lay down the ego and you'll be okay. I'm here to tell you that you're my best friend and that like it or not, you are stuck with me forever. So I'm done. I'm done fighting. And push me away all you want, but I'm not leaving.

I was wrong
and I swear,
I'm going to stop quoting lyrics to hurt you.

I've been putting off writing this. I repeat it in my head, but I know you're not talking to me right now. It's scary to go through all these emotions not knowing what I can do about them. But pushing them down until I forget they exist is what got us here in the first place.

I am so, so, sorry. Sorry doesn't even begin to express the absolute remorse that I feel. You came back and said everything you had to say, and I wasn't able to process it right then. It turns out that I had been stuck for months in the hurt that I felt back in December. Thinking I was "fine without you." Proving I was "fine without you," felt like what I needed to do. I put on a show, even for myself. Instead of processing the pain, I pushed it so far down that I didn't even know it was all still there. When you came back, it brought all of the emotions back too, and at that point it was more than just missing you. It was more than hurt and sad. It was rage in it's purest form. Expressing that rage set me free. Everything I had harbored from trying so damn hard to be perfect, to not be hurt. Once unleashed, I could feel the sad again. I could let go of my ego, because the truth is, I had already forgiven you. I was just scared of being hurt again and easily triggered back into the original wound. These feelings took control of my actions. I'm so sorry for all of this. I'm sorry this has gone on for so long. I'm sorry for trying to hurt you. I'm so sorry that I was not able to meet you halfway when you came to me with an apology. I wasn't ready, but I'm ready now. I miss you more than words can describe. More than anything I want to be close to you again and I'm sorry that my actions didn't show that. I hope that you can forgive me. I hope that we can make it through this.

To the moon and back,

Abigail

102

There came a point in time
that I became so intoxicated by your presence,
every time I saw your face,
I found a bottle in my hand.
The first time,
was the last time I reached out.
And in return I got the one thing
I wanted more than anything.
We hugged and cried and forgave.
But I can't fully remember it.

- Complications with liquid courage.

YEARNING
(Can I make this enough?)

I sit here in front of you,
wondering why I still hurt.
Because as much as I love you,
I miss when you and I were made of magic.

Because I love you,
and I am addicted to
the memory
of how loved
you once made me feel.

My therapist wants to know why
I still keep you around.
I tell her I don't know,
because I can't bring myself to
explain even to her,
of all of the ways
that I want you around.
     - I've never had a relationship that costs so much.

I'm scared to write this. To allow it into existence, when I don't know that I want it here at all. But in all truth... I don't think that admitting it makes it any more or less real. And honestly, there's a good chance I'm going to tear out these pages and burn them to destroy any evidence of them existing at all. So here goes nothing.

Right before the beginning of the end, I began to wonder if you loved me differently. A little more... than I loved you. It's true that being loved by you taught me that I was sunshine. But I couldn't help but wonder if that was due to maybe, a little extra sparkle in your eyes.

It's true that back then I didn't, couldn't, love you like that. Whether my assumptions were right or not.

But, it's just as true that I still remember the first time you whispered in my ear back in middle school and it sent shivers through my spine and down my legs. That was before we were even friends.

There was some point between our falling out, coming back together, and now... that those shivers came back. The rejection I felt when you didn't appreciate my touch. The fantasies I've made up in my head feel so real in my body that I can't make an excuse. The jealousy I feel when you tell me about another girl that makes you feel something.

And yet, I still wonder if my deep yearning to be close to you has lead me to a craving that feels more within reach than the emotional intimacy you so obscenely deject... a craving for your touch. Your outward admiration for me that I imagine I could extract from your bones, instead of a love in your heart you speak of, yet can't show.

If I spent so much time loving you so deeply, yet in no ways but one, why do I feel like this now? It is an insatiable lust that wants only one thing... a vulnerable love.

What if it's all in my head? What if your feelings never

expanded and I am the one unable to accept my own? Wanting to gently seduce you, so as not to expose a secret that you may or may not want.

One thing is for sure, everything in me is telling me not to cross that line. But then I think of your touch. A love I crave so much. And the line seems to blur.

I think we got drunk all of those nights hoping that a lucid craving would take all of the inhibitions away. Maybe that was just me. Maybe I'm just so deep in denial that I can't admit it.

I want you as more than a best friend.

Maybe,
all of the love
you didn't like when I expressed,
needed somewhere else to go.
     - Ashes to ashes.
      Love to lust.

Because we are friends...
who are only affectionate when were drunk.
Who know each other's every turn on
and exactly where we like to be touched.
And I might enjoy when you play with my hair
just a little too much.
And I can't look you in the eyes for more than three seconds,
as if one second too many
and the butterflies might escape,
exposing everything.
Maybe it's all in my head
and I'm making it all up.
But then again,
I know you have a tendency
for falling in love too easily,
and that you've developed feelings for
every close friend you've ever had.
But I can't risk something
that may end in losing you.
If we could do this,
and when it's all over
make our friendship still work,
I'd confess right now.
Instead...
No more than three seconds
and all touch must be minimal.
I'll hardly say I love you,
even though I want to.

>   - Thought streams of the confused, conflicted, and
>   concealing.

Maybe,
I needed a reason
to convince myself
it wasn't a self-betrayal
when I stopped
expressing my love.

It's the slight smirk we both share
every time we get a little too close.
The stillness in the air between,
before we've had enough time
to let go of the breath that caught,
just knowing our lips
could be so conveniently near.

I think we are trying to make
a platonic relationship
out of non-platonic feelings.
Creating a circle of boundaries
that is bigger than the normal circle
around two friends.
Because we don't know how to be just that.

> - Or maybe, I'm just trying to make sense of the way
> you are willing to love me.

I wonder if we finally gave in just once,
(Do you have something that you want to give in to?)
if this would all be so hard.
I wonder if we finally gave in,
if our lips could heal what sharp words started.

Once, you helped me into a corset, and I asked if undressing in front of you was okay. But I wondered to myself if it was okay that I wanted to undress in front of so badly. As you did up the back I held my breath, not to be smaller, but to hide how much I liked your fingers grazing my bare skin. That, and holding your breath always feels like a good idea in moments that you don't want to forget. Like my frozen breath could help imprint the feeling of your touch as you weaved the laces through. I always found my lip within my teeth in quiet moments around you. Like my body was trying to remind me that I shouldn't ache to fill the silence with all of the ways that I want you.

Once, the pull got so strong, that laying on a bed next to you hurt in the absolute best way. I couldn't stand being so close to you and not touching. The idea of it made my voice go soft, but my body stiff from holding back so fiercely. I always hoped the softness of my voice would signal to you how much I wanted you to soften my body too.

Once, I got drunk and danced around naked as you tried to convince me to get dressed. I don't remember this, but years later I got drunk and asked you if you had thought it was cute. Maybe I always had feelings for you, and just finally got tired of hiding it.

Once, a stranger noticed the way I lit up around you and interpreted it as deep feelings, but applied them to the wrong person. I made a joke of it the best I could, but I'm sure you suspected. After that I knew I had to tell you or hide it a lot better.

Once, with a shy energy, you rambled about how you *kind of like anyone who gives you attention* and I said, *I get flare-ups of that condition too.* We paused, eyes locked. For a split second, it sounded like we were leading up to our confessional. But my heart raced straight to my head, changing the subject before anything else could be said. I guess I was terrified too.

Once, we got drunk in an overly expensive hotel room and I told you I didn't want to sleep in different beds. We soaked our feet in the bath tub together, but I couldn't stop thinking about how it could accommodate a lot more than our feet. Leaving a trail of wet footprints, shirts, and empty bottles, we moved to the couch and moaned as we massaged each other. That night I learned for certain that the only straight thing about me, is how I like my vodka.

Once, we sat in a car together for hours. Talking and laughing from sunrise to sunset as we crossed state line after line. Maybe, if I had known it back then, things would be different now. But, I'd never take falling in love a different way. In our own little bubble, passing the world by. So gentle and natural that I didn't even recognize it for what it was.

Once, I watched you put your hand on her knee. I tried to hide the visceral doubling-over reaction my body wanted to have. Instead, my eyes immediately darted over to the side the second you looked at me. That probably said more than if I had just continued to watch.

Once, we both began to speak more and more about the men who could have our hearts. But really, the only person I wanted to give mine to, *was you*.

Once, I asked you if you thought love was enough. You said no, and I agreed. But knowing you were the reason I agreed, I didn't ask you to explain your answer. I was too afraid I was your reason too.

Once, we were able to say I love you. And that's when we fell apart.

Inspired by Trista Mateer, Barefoot Molly

I wonder if pressing my lips to your neck
could help you let go enough
that you'd stop trying so hard to hide yourself in front of me.
I wonder if I could help you release and relax
that way that I did every time you touched me.

Is it because you didn't want me,
that I was so eager to give myself away?
Would I still want you,
if you wanted me too?

When other people began to see it,
I knew I had to do something.
I told myself I had to choose:
Tell you,
or make these feelings disappear.

- I've always been indecisive

Maybe,
I like the idea
of carrying a secret,
that I wonder,
if once handed to you,
could miraculously finally
make me feel loved by you.
Like there is still something I could do
to make this easier for you.

      - As you walk away I'll whisper, *if only you knew.*

Maybe,
my love for you was so true,
it had all the capacity
to expand into something more.
- It was suspicious that it decided now was the time.

Hardly able to find the letters I type out,
I'm in love with you.
But then meticulously press back,
so as not to hit send.

Maybe,
I'm trying to change my love
to better fit
what it is that you think you need.

Maybe,
in my head
is the only place
I know how to keep you.

That night (what I would have hoped was her perspective):

I heard how you wanted me in the gentle crisp sigh
you let slip out as my fingertips grazed
down the edge of your ear to your neck.
I heard the multiplying shallow breaths you took as my palms
shaped the skin on your naked back.
I know you didn't mean to turn me on like this,
but I adored when we switched,
and you tugged on my hair.
I could hear the playfulness in your voice,
but I'm sorry,
because although your hands had my full attention,
your words did not.
Your fingers raked through my hair
and slid down to my shoulders
not stopping until you were pressing into skin near my spine.
But your hands lost all of their leverage as I began to imagine
everything that wasn't touching me.
I ached for your lips on my neck.
For you to tell me how I taste.
For your hands to slip a little lower.
The warmth of your breath to come a little closer
as you whispered in my ear.

> *Dear god,*
> *I even ached for your breath.*

Maybe,
your refusal
for physical affection,
made me want your touch even more.

Or maybe,
I fell in love before I wrote that first letter.
Maybe, getting lost on winding roads
was inspiration enough.
And I just didn't know how tight
the grip you had on me was...
until you let go.

> - I was always a bleeding heart, but it seemed like less of
>   a problem when it was held by you.

I'm scared that when you find out how I want you
the opportunity will present itself,
to finally show you,
what wanting you feels like.
But, I'm scared that it'll mean more to me
than it ever did to you.
And you'll break my heart again.
I'm always scared you'll break my heart again.

You are still the only person
who feels like utterly understood me.
Though this person doesn't seem to be you now...
I choose to believe she's still in there somewhere.
I still want to share every little thing with you.
Things that I know no one else is going to quite understand
in the way that I want them to.
You are still the person I want to bring my excitement to.
The person I want to bring my joy to.
The person I want to bring my love to.
The person I want to bring my sadne–
It's hard to share in only the pleasant.
And the you I know today,
can't even share in that anymore.

Part of loving you meant wanting to share new things with you.
But you look at me like I'm a foreign country
and you're terrified of new cities.
I always dreamed of taking you to new places,
I never thought that convincing you to come with me
would be the insurmountable feat.

Maybe that is the difference,
between platonic and romantic love.
Envisioning a future I long for.

Sometimes I still have dreams of running away with that girl.
Maybe a far off land is the only place that there can be a you and me.

I will never understand
how you can stand here
and reject all of the love
that I want to give you.
I would give you the absolute world.
I would bleed myself dry.
The things I wouldn't do for a person like me.
All I want is for you to turn around
and love me hard too.

     - Irony.

Maybe,
I began to feel
my own love for you
slipping away.

    - I tried so hard to get it back.

    But you weren't you anymore.

You said I made you feel like
you were doing too little.
And you always said that
I was too much.
I guess neither of us knew
how to be
just enough.

ENOUGH.
(I've had enough.)

If I remember correctly,
getting high together for the first time
was your idea.
I should have been more afraid of you
than I was of any substance.
No one ever taught me
it could be a person
that was the gateway to addiction.

I am going to lose me,
if I don't change something
about the way that
I allow myself to love you.

I'm running towards you
with an empty cup,
because you make it feel full again.
You're running away
with a cup so full,
every time I fill it,
it spills over.
We make each other
face and feel ourselves.
You fear the way
that I make you feel.
I am obsessed with the way
that you make me feel.
                - The anxious and the avoidant.

"Through your eyes,"
cannot be my favorite way
to see myself.

Is it the open wounds,
or the scars,
that you want people to see so badly?
- We were never victims.

The weight of trying to keep you
is heavier than the weight
of losing you.
I'm okay with losing you now.
Do you hear me?!
I'm not going to be here forever.

You say you miss me.
You say you love me.
You gift me old pictures of us,
seemingly to exhibit your reminiscence.
For a moment I fall for it.
But you only want me when you want to.

- Loving me isn't supposed to be a chore.

You finally appreciate me wearing my heart on my sleeve.
I am bringing myself to cry in front of you again.
To let you see all of the pain you are causing me.
Knowing damn well,
how predictable your next move is.
Feeling hurt is not manipulative.
Telling you I'm hurt
is not manipulation.

I am not guilting you.
You simply feel guilty.
And if you leave again,
I'm not going to let you convince me it was my fault.

Love sees it all
and still chooses you.
Admiration sees what it wants
and chooses love.

I thought I had to prove my healing
by being unaffected by the things
that once hurt me.

        - There is no amount of growing you can do that will
          trick your heart into still beating the same while it
          bleeds.

I never told you,
but I finally let you go.
You didn't want me to beg
and I didn't want you to leave.
But I finally stopped trying so hard to keep you,
when you couldn't keep me.

It's not that you didn't deserve my love.
It's just that I deserved love in return.
I wanted you to appreciate my love.
And you didn't.

  - You deserve all of the love in the world. It just can't be
    mine.

When I stopped letting you
walk all over me,
you stopped coming around as much.
I guess that was the only place
you knew where to step.

I tried to prove my love
by refusing to walk away.
But let it be known,
I have never felt so much love
than within this single act.

      - Loving yourself isn't selfish.

My power is not in hiding
how you hurt me.
My power is in refusing
to be hurt by you again.
Until you lay down the sword,
I have no interest in communicating with you.

You told me that you just didn't show me
all of the ways you loved me.
I pretended that wasn't true.
You knew it too.

   - I don't know why I stayed so long.

Maybe we were never meant to be lovers,
but when our dance as friends seemed over,
god how I wanted to try.
   - I was once willing to try anything.

I'd kiss you with chapped lips.
Hold you with shaking arms.
And love you with a broken heart.
          - I am not her anymore.

I've learned that I don't have to be
the sole source of my happiness,
and that loving myself doesn't mean
not wanting you to love me too.
It's like knowing
and appreciating the stars,
regardless of how many of them can be seen.
Because in some places,
the view is simply better.
The stars appear brighter
and in infinite abundance.

You were one of those places.
And I'm okay with that now.

I expected too much
from you.
I expected you to return a love
like the one I gave freely.
A love you never asked for.

You can't change people
who don't fit your expectations.
But you can choose to let in
only the people that do.

The more that you heal,
the more that you are able to feel.
The more you stretch into
experiencing and releasing the pain,
the more you can expand into
the ability to feel joyful bliss.

   - The rubber band.

None of this was ever about me.
Your leaving.
Your unkind words.
Your inability to express yourself.
Your quick to replace nature.
None of it defines who I am.
You don't define me.

It's like I'm stretching the grief,
because it's all I have left.

I think about you all the time. I wonder if what I'm doing is right. If it's right for me. If these actions align with the person I want to be. I'm not giving you any of my attention. Not texting you. Not acknowledging the short videos you share with me. It's been almost a month since we've spoken. This time, there was no explosion or grand goodbye. I actually tried talking to you. Respected when you didn't want to talk, but that can't last forever. I kept making myself the "bigger person." I'm beginning to recognize that that just looked like less needs to you. You turned every one of my emotions against me. You are so scared of your own feelings, that you thought all of mine were wrong too. I don't feel bad about them anymore. They all have something to say, and I trust them now.

You've been popping up in my dreams again. A lot. And I wonder if it's you thinking about me... I think some dreams are our psyche working through all of our unconscious hurt. But I also wonder if there is a dream plane that is different from the world that we know, and if it's easier to manipulate. Maybe sometimes we meet each other here. In this place, we are softer. Not bloody or bruised. In this place, we don't have to do or say anything to be what we need. In this place, our souls can collide as our humans rest.

Maybe losing me will finally hurt,
when you know just how much,
I loved you.

       - I don't want to like knowing it hurts you (but god just
         for a minute I want to know this meant something to
         you too and believe it).

I know I said I let you go,
but some wave has come back for me.
The moon it seems has demanded,
that I not be left behind.
I am not going down with you.

Sometimes I still imagine
what it would feel like to have your lips
pressed against mine.
I imagine they would be warm and delicate and taste of grapes.
And with the swirling of tongues we could slowly
press and crush,
and turn all that we share into fine Verona wine.
I imagine your voice,
soft and smooth,
as I twist my fingers into your hair
and we indulge in the sweetness.

But that fantasy expires quickly,
and shatters
like Cinderella's dropped glass slipper.
Because for any of this to work out,
we'd have to age together.

I want to believe in fairy-tale endings again.

There was maybe a month,
in which you completely drew me in.
Loving me without withholding.
Letting me love you without running.
I would come back to this month.
Replaying.
Rereading.
Wondering if any of it was real.

> \- I guess it didn't matter if it was real or not—
> I loved you either way.

Every phone buzz.
Doorbell ring.
Beat up and bumper stickered silver little car.
I hope they are all you.
And then I pray that they aren't.

I still really hope
that although this book is for me,
that you'll read it.
That it will all make sense now.
And me loving you too will be enough
for you to come back.
But, these aren't conditions I am okay with.
You don't get to love me just because I love you.
I don't want there to be potential
within the idea that
the more love I give you,
the more likely you will be to finally return to me.
I don't want to bask in moon beams
if I have to cure myself of all light
in order for them to reach me.
I'm tired of sitting in the dark,
waiting for you to come find me.

Isn't it interesting how we all share the same air,
yet find so much romance in sharing the same breath?
The chances we have shared the same air,
and thusly the same breath,
are slim.
But, enough that I don't dare move to a new city,
so as not to lessen the possibility
that we might.

      - I don't want to interfere with fate.

I lived for those messages you sent
while I was trying to ignore you.
Trying to stick to my boundaries.
If you weren't willing to talk things through,
I couldn't keep giving you all of my energy while I was hurting.
But every rectangle illusion
that everything was okay,
satisfied the tension of thirst.
Finally,
I didn't have to beg for your attention.
I never responded.
But god,
I was living for those messages.

The only reason I knew you saw my final text was because after I
sent it, those grace saving droplets ceased completely.
And you were back to pretending I don't exist.

What if the next person I love makes our love feel less special?
What if the next person I love heals my heart so thoroughly,
(because this is what's meant to come next right?)
that all of the pin pricks of pain
that are keeping the ways I loved you
posted to my heart,
come undone.
And I am never able to truly recall what loving you was like.

What if you didn't love me like that? What if this book makes you want to announce a declaration of how gross and messy and unkind you think I am for ever even thinking of you like that. What if it makes you want to declare your lack of love for me. The way you never saw me like that. What if this gives you the power to break my heart again? What if I believe you when you say you never loved me, just like I didn't believed you when you said you did?

What if...?

What if...?

What if...?

But then I remind myself, avoiding me is your middle name, and you probably won't ever read these words.

I still want your love so bad,
that just the simple idea of you being happy
makes my whole body erupt with rage.
How can you laugh at a time like this?
Losing me should hurt more than that.

I am of a forgiving nature.
A kind creature.
A compassionate creature.
One may even call me a *sweet creature*.
But you have abused that time and time again,
and now all I hold towards you is anger.
I tried so hard not to hate you.
But fighting myself is worse than fighting with you.
I can't stand the thought of you.
And I am going to revel in that.

It is beyond frustrating that you can just pretend like I don't exist. That I never existed. Beyond frustrating that you can turn off all of your emotions when you turn mine on like a garbage disposal. Flipping to life, spitting and swirling. Until every single one is gnawing at the thought of pulverizing all memory of you, just so that I can sound like myself again.

Some days, I wish I could hollow myself out and just play pretend too.

Did Prince Charming come and save you yet?
I know you've been waiting,
and that a man was written in the cards.
But trust me on this one...
Even I couldn't save you from yourself.
That Prince-Charming-Knight-in-Shining-Armor doesn't exist.

A healthy person would just apologize.
A healthy person would just apologize.
A healthy person would just apologize.
    - You didn't have to hurt me to defend yourself.
    I held a shield. You held the sword.

You learned that you fixate on people,
that's nice sunshine...
Is that why she's more important than me?
Please,
keep making excuses for all the reasons you're hurting me.

Saying you love me,
while knowingly continuing to hurt me—
honey,
that's what they call manipulation.

You're right,
I was jealous.
But why did you have to weaponize it like it was so bad?
Was it that you had to deal with the guilt,
as you watched the hurt you drowned me in,
rise to my eyes?
I didn't know it then,
but I think it all started with
when you told me,
if she wanted you,
you were sure you'd want her too.

I got drunk and sobbed uncontrollably for hours to a sad song on repeat over the memory of you last night. I knew within the madness there was still something to lose.

- Anger is a secondary emotion.

I felt so loved when—

I kept humming the song that was stuck in my head, and so you started playing it aloud for me to sing to.

You told me how you noticed on the bad days I wear that sweatshirt from New York.

I was having a really bad day, nearly silent, and you covered me in a blanket while I wrote.

You sat and cried with me as I broke for reasons I can't explain.

You defended me. Again, and again, and again.

You brought me surprise "just because" gifts. All of the time.

You called me. Every. Single. Day.

You took photos of me every time I asked. And god, I asked a lot.

You cried at the simple thought of me happy.

You planned picnics and birthdays and trips for the two of us.

You played with my hair whenever I was sitting within reach.

You looked me up and down after months of back and forth and opened your arms as if you knew that was the one thing I needed more than anything.

- The memories in question.

Now you are:

A box under my bed.

My favorite broken heart.

A book on my shelf.

A record player.

The song *All Too Well*.

Everything Halloween.

Dogs.

Fairy lights.

A handwritten note on a card I'll never be able to throw away.

A pebble from the ocean that sometimes I wear around my neck.

Late night drives.

Hundreds of bittersweet photos.

The person I miss most everytime I travel somewhere new.

Waterfalls.

Nutmeg.

Tapestries.

Roller coasters.

Ivy vines.

The reason I won't ever be able to enjoy watching the movie

Madagascar again.

Hotel rooms.

Paint.

Tiled floors.

Purple grapes.

Soup.

Card games.

Hummingbirds.

Fall.

The girl I loved more than anything else.

It took me a lot longer
than I'd like to admit,
to fully confess to myself how much I loved you.
And even longer for me to fully accept it.
I was comfortable admitting my sexuality
and knew it was you who awakened it.
But god forbid
I admitted to the fact that
I loved you
long before I hated you.

Would I go back and do it over again?

If I could love her one more time and snap back to today, abso-
lutely. But if it meant reliving it all again, honestly there is no
chance in hell. And I think that is an attestation to how I view self-
love. I love who I am today. But, if I had been given the choice of a
magic pill to change me overnight, or the years of heartbreak that
damn near killed me, I'd choose the magic pill. Yes, I love her. Yes,
I want to share that love with her again. But it is out of love that I
don't. It is out of love that I refuse the thing I want most, knowing
it would be a suicide mission. Love shouldn't kill you.

She was the person who shattered my fairy-tale heart. She once described me as, "not a glass half-full, nor half-empty" kind of person, but an, "at least there is a glass" kind of person. I don't know that I feel like that anymore. And it terrifies me. I don't believe in true love the way that I used to and I want to. God how I want to. I'm worried if I don't believe in it, it won't ever happen. What if what made it real was my belief that it exists. Maybe it can be real, and I just don't know it yet.

- At least there is a glass.

I keep wondering if any of this was real.
If I could be convincing myself of feelings that weren't true.
But, I've never written a love letter for anyone else.
Or felt for anyone what I felt for you.
Or known where any of my other friends
like to be touched.
Or remembered where any of my other friends
like to be touched.
Never have I told anyone else about all of the people that could
have my heart, in order to deflect the hurt from hearing the list
of people who could have yours.
Never has anyone else told me that being around me felt too
intense.

*I don't have to intellectualize this as if I'm already preparing myself for
the explanation, in case I'm asked for an apology.
Because the truth is,
I don't have to know when,
or why.
I won't apologize for loving you the way that I did.*

I'm scared if I fall in love with a man,
after having loved you,
I will never be able to prove
whether I was truly in love with you or not.

- Honey, next to you or not, a man isn't proof.

What if the pain is what is making it feel real?
What if I can never relate to our story again?
Maybe that's why I needed to write the book—
to remember me,
next to you.

Because it's time I finally let her go.

I keep imagining what it will be like,
when the inevitable happens
and I see you again.
Will you avoid my gaze?
And if you don't, what will be the expression in your eyes?
Love, melancholy, fear, longing, rage?
If I had to guess,
it would be fear.
It's hard to upkeep avoidance with someone in the same space.
Too bad I can't end our story myself.
But for now,
I'm closing the book.

I don't know if I always loved you like that.
But, a part of me believes that the truest of loves
are the ones that always existed.
Love at first sight.
Then again, maybe it's just that a love this strong,
makes me forget a time when I didn't love you.
It feels nearly impossible to imagine a life like that.

I spent a long time
wanting love from another person.
Trying to procure love from the bones of a body
that wasn't mine.
And you know what?
The only person who's love I could guarantee was my own.
I refuse to spend another day hating,
or questioning myself,
when I am the only person
whose love I can guarantee.

I want you to tell me that it's okay.
That you love me,
and you know I love you too.
Give me permission to take the good,
and leave the bad.
Tell me that this wasn't all just one big cosmic lesson.
Tell me you don't want to forget.
Tell me this was all worth it.
Tell me that I still mean something to you.
Tell me you'll still hold our memories fondly
and that I don't have to do it alone anymore.
I'm so tired of begging,
so this is the last time I'll ask but–
Please.
      Please.
Tell me it's okay to let go.

How do I even ask for a goodbye? How do I say: *I think this is actually it for us... at least for many years to come.*

"Hey. Can you remind me why we aren't talking? *(since I never told you the true reason I couldn't be around you anymore and of all the ways in which you were breaking my heart.)* Anyway, no matter the reason, I don't think we are good for each other right now. But I miss the hell out of you. So I'd like to say goodbye, and maybe finally move on. Could we say goodbye in person?"

"Hi. I'm about to publish that book and there's something in there I'd really like to confess to you one-on-one, before you hear it from other people... also kinda hoping this will be it for us... because I can't take this heartbreak anymore. Maybe we could talk? Give ourselves a goodbye?"

"Hey! I wished you a happy birthday just a few days ago and honestly thought I would at least get a drunken, "fuck you" reply. Anyways... Do you miss me like I miss you? Do you feel like no matter how much you want to and how hard you try, you still can't drag yourself to move on? Well boy do I have the trick for you! One day only (if today works for you, haha) deal! Let's meet up and say goodbye one last time. 71.7% chance guarantee to relieve a broken heart."

"Hi. Can we talk? Just wondering if the 5 months of zero communication cured me of my feelings and we might have a chance at being friends again? Then again, we'd also need to see if you're over the whole avoidance thing... And if we can be within 5 feet of each other without immediately needing to become intoxicated. We really were the definition of toxic, weren't we? Wanna relive it one last time?"

The reply:

"   "

A disappearing act wasn't the magic I wanted.

HERE LIES US
(A eulogy for you and me)

Today, we lay to rest two people that lost their lives to broken hearts. Sacrificed the people that they were in the name of true love. May they get a life together in some other world. May the versions of them that are gone never spend another day without the other. May they get the life that they always wanted.

May the versions of them who stayed rise, shedding only feathers now. As a result of the loss they endured so courageously, may they be able to love with the depth of the Mariana Trench and with the strength of elephant feet beating on broken earth. May they also get the life that they always wanted. May they get to say goodbye to the love of their life in whatever way they need so that they may be able to put that love somewhere else. May dirt fill the cracks in their hearts so that new love may grow. May they put that love into their own hearts first, and when they have extra, may they give that to the people that they care about most. May love never hurt like that again. May they rest in peace.

Dear Annie,

I wish that you'd give me the chance to say goodbye. I wish I would feel okay asking. But now I've told people my final sign would be saying goodbye to you, because there is not a chance in hell I'd leave this earth without hearing your voice one more time. So maybe I should thank you, for literally making saying goodbye so hard.

Maybe it's my mind deceiving me, but today—today I just want to say goodbye so that I can let the old me go and the new me flourish. I know hanging onto you is holding me back. I need to let the part of me that loved you go. But I don't know how to keep going without a final goodbye. One we both can mean. One in which we both can cry and thank each other for everything. One we can say *I love you and I hate you and I'm sorry, but this is just the way that it is.* One we both know the other needs as much as ourselves. One that gives us closure and the "I love you's," and "I wish you the best's," so that we may take only the joy with us as we leave. One that allows us to go on with our lives. One that catches us both up, so that we may fade apart again. One that is both a confession and a prayer. One that lets a part of me die and be reborn again. I wonder what it is that I need from this conversation that I can't give to myself… and it's simply just you. Because I don't need an apology or forgiveness. I just want to hold you one last time and say goodbye. In a world that it seems everyone someday leaves… can we acknowledge the loss even if we can't go back? Can't we give ourselves that?

Let's say goodbye like we mean it. Like this may possibly be the last time we will ever see each other again. At least leaving for good would give me an excuse to say goodbye like this. I don't know how to ask for a goodbye that doesn't feel completely real. I don't want to ask for a goodbye without knowing how it would make you feel. But if I did, and we could, let's say goodbye like this:

Let's say goodbye like we aren't going to come back. Let's say goodbye like I will miss you always, but this has to be it.

Let's say goodbye like we don't know what tomorrow will bring, but there can't be check-ins every time it rains. Let's say goodbye like, I'm not going to text you happy birthday or condolences or thinking of you… But instead, I offer them now. Because I will never forget your birthday and there won't ever be a time that I don't think of you, especially on this day. And every time I miss you, I will try to send you all of the love in the heart. And I'll admit, there likely won't ever be a day I don't miss you. Let me tell you that today, so that maybe I won't feel the need to tell you for the rest of my life. Let's acknowledge the need to move on and the amount of pain it would cause to stay in touch, even in the little ways. Let's say, "I don't know why" and maybe even play the game of "what if." Then let's hug and cry and laugh like it's our last day on Earth. Let's watch as the only sun and moon we have each ever known explodes and falls. And one day, each of us will find a new Earth, a new Sun, a new Moon. And that will be our home.

I can't explain to you how much I want to tell you about this book. I can't explain to you the peace it would bring me if we could share in this experience together. How I wish I could text you I miss you and you could text me it too and we could both acknowledge how deeply sad we are and then sit together knowing that at least we agree. We can't meet with where we are.

Letting you go does not mean forgetting.
It just means I don't need the pain anymore to remember.
Let all these pages be the placeholder.

I stopped hoping you'd come back.
Because you've come back before,
and that hasn't done us any good.
Instead I'm letting you go,
and I'm making a wish:
I hope you change.
I hope it's for the better.
And then I hope
we meet again.

I admire how you refuse to let this experience rob you of the rest of your life. I'm still learning how to do that. And I admire your dedication to preserving the good by not dragging out the stain of bad. And if I had to guess, you probably still only speak of me with pretty words. Sometimes, I wish I could say I do the same. I admire how you can choose easy, when easy is what you need.

- Reframing those shattered frames.

I still miss you,
but I don't know that the person I miss
exists right now.
I still love you,
but I don't think that the person who can accept this love
is you anymore.
Now that I've worked through everything else,
I'm back to missing you.
But this time it's pure.
This time I will grieve that girl fully.
Because this time I know,
though you may change,
you are never going back.
I will never see her again.

    - I hope you change for the better.

(Now read it again, but this time for yourself.)

It is unfortunate,
yet fittingly poetic.
The way I've found myself writing my first ever book,
with the end of you and me.
This is how we were meant to be
a story told.

I tried to change around you,
thinking I could make myself easier to love.
Now that I've changed without you,
and see that you are still the same,
I truly believe,
it is a
blind-eyed-unwillingness to evolve,
that makes love
not enough.

This.
This really is the final letter.

My life has finally started moving again. I watched that movie we were going to watch together. I finally visited the place that I was saving for a trip with you. I can listen to the music that I know made you think of me, and find nostalgia instead of resentment. I've begun to finally tell my friends how I really felt about you. How I think I may have always loved you more than either of us was ready for. How it hurt like hell, how losing you was absolute hell. You were the moon to my sun, and the sun to my moon. I really did love you and maybe love doesn't have to be forever...

Maybe forever love isn't about where two people stand. But the spark that they ignited together. Maybe a love like that doesn't always live in hearts. Maybe it escapes and is a force to be reckoned with, working magic in ways we aren't able to predict. Maybe you were a forever kind of love, whether we always feel it or not. I hope you find truth in this too.

I will always be angry with the girl who broke my heart. I don't think that negates how mended my heart feels now. A part of me will always remember how screwed up it was to be loved in absolute consumption, and then having it completely ripped away. My mind may always hold echoes of the whispers in my stomach that wondered if any of it was real. I may never know how you truly felt. Which voice was true: the one that said she believed we would have something grand again, or the one that screamed at me to stop treating her like my boyfriend? But, these questions no longer carry a captive heart. I know my heart is mended not by a lack of anger, but by the lack of control that it holds. I don't need to know how you felt, and actually I prefer it this way. I don't need to focus on knowing you anymore. This was always about knowing me.

And what I know now is this:

I loved you. I loved you as my best friend. And I also had

deep feelings for you, whether I was always aware of them or not. Whether you loved me the same or not. It wasn't until I was losing you as my best friend that I needed you more than that. I believe we were never meant to be more, at least not right now. I also believe we were always supposed to fall apart.

A part of me will always hate the way you made me feel, this is the part of me that knows I didn't deserve that. A part of me will always be grateful for the way that you made me feel, this is the part of me that knows I deserve to feel that every day. Both, the anger and the gratitude, have found warmth in loving me. Both were screaming in their own ways for me to allow myself to be found. It's okay that I loved you in the way that I did. It's okay that it expanded. It's okay that I lost myself when I lost you. I can take what I've learned and all the love too. Although you had a lesson to teach me, you were so much more than just that. I know now, that I could handle the heartbreak should it happen again (whether it be with you or someone else). I know now that I can love with a capacity I never thought possible. I know now that I can let myself be loved in a way that once felt too tucked in fear to be found. I know now what I'm okay with and what I'm not when it comes to the actions and words of other people. I know now that I can walk away instead of being consumed by the need to be loved, to be known, to be seen, to be worthy. I can walk away because my sense of self is no longer tied to it. Maybe love isn't enough... but we were. This was enough. We were enough.

Even after all of this,
my heart circles back to the
teary-eyed-golden-light-grateful feeling
that engulfs me,
just at the thought of us.
Because how can I be anything but loving of something that forced
me to find myself.
Maybe this is how it was meant to be.

    - I am enough.

Acknowledgements

A special thank you to all of the people on my journey that have read every word of every edit and expressed all of the emotions that each line brought up. This encouraged me on my path to publishing more than you know. Thank you to everyone who loved me unconditionally and shared in my excitement. Thank you for helping me to find the confidence to share my voice with the world.

Thank you reader, for buying this book and taking part in this journey with me. It's you who makes my voice feel so big. I've always dreamed of being a writer, and in some ways it feels I always have. But, it's you who reads these words that brings it to life. With so much gratitude and love, thank you, thank you, thank you.

About the author

Abigail Culbertson is a newly published author with her title, Enough, being her debut book. Abigail has spent every day since she could write journaling, and began writing poetry in high school. With a love for adventure, she has found herself studying Earthships in the New Mexico Desert, assisting in rehabbing wildlife in the foothills of the Rocky Mountains, caring for rescued farm animals in the Finger Lakes region of New York, exploring cities all over the world, starting craft businesses for fun, and studying marketing on a whim.

Currently calling Colorado home, she hopes to continue to travel and fall in love on road trips, eagerly awaiting sharing it through more books with all of you.

Lightning Source UK Ltd.
Milton Keynes UK
UKHW020722060922
408420UK00009B/460